T0123526

THE MIND OF THE DEPRESSED

MY LIFE, MY STORY

TRISTAN JAMES

iUniverse®

THE MIND OF THE DEPRESSED
MY LIFE, MY STORY

Copyright © 2018 Tristan James.

All rights reserved. No part of this book may be used or reproduced by any means, graphic, electronic, or mechanical, including photocopying, recording, taping or by any information storage retrieval system without the written permission of the author except in the case of brief quotations embodied in critical articles and reviews.

iUniverse books may be ordered through booksellers or by contacting:

iUniverse
1663 Liberty Drive
Bloomington, IN 47403
www.iuniverse.com
1-800-Authors (1-800-288-4677)

Because of the dynamic nature of the Internet, any web addresses or links contained in this book may have changed since publication and may no longer be valid. The views expressed in this work are solely those of the author and do not necessarily reflect the views of the publisher, and the publisher hereby disclaims any responsibility for them.

Any people depicted in stock imagery provided by Getty Images are models, and such images are being used for illustrative purposes only.
Certain stock imagery © Getty Images.

ISBN: 978-1-5320-5309-2 (sc)
ISBN: 978-1-5320-5310-8 (e)

Library of Congress Control Number: 2018910118

Print information available on the last page.

iUniverse rev. date: 09/26/2018

This book is dedicated to my mother and for every other loving mother. My heart is full of the love you gave and, for you, I will love and live the best I can.

Your ever-loving son.

To the rest of all my fellow suffers, you are not alone, you are loved.

CONTENTS

PROLOGUE

I AM WRITING ABOUT DEPRESSION, not to sell a million books, but because it is something that I truly believe in. Something that I have lived with since the age of five, and I am now fifty years old. It isn't because I want to make my story understood, but because I want to make the effects of the disease called Depression better understood. There are many states of depression and of course, we are all afflicted with some level of depression. The problem is ignorance. I am going to tell you about my life story, because I know I have lived in a depressive state, from a young age. I hid it from myself, family, friends and loved ones. It was much easier, in my mind, to leave it festering, without ever coming out and because of my ignorance, I allowed it to grow and create a moment of inertia that, at times, left destructive paths.

Letting everyone know, by writing this book, is the hardest thing I have ever done. I am not only admitting it to myself, but to everyone else that I have lived with, in this depressed state, throughout most of my life. There is no other way then to dive deep into my story. I make absolutely no claims, in any way, to be a professional analyst and or to have any medical degree. It is simply the story of my life. I'm here to write my story, the battle of my depressive life, how depression affected me and how it affected everyone else that crossed my path. I have not only been destructive to my own life, but to the people that I care about most. Their complete understanding and endless support made me wish that I was capable of battling my affliction of depression, earlier in my life.

CHAPTER ONE

THE WORLD OF THE DEPRESSED IS THE life I have lived. It has been a struggle, in my case, from a very young age. I took great effort just getting through the simply things that most take for granted, like waking up and wanting to go out the door. I recall the pains, not only in my mind, but the aches that I felt in my bones. I recall walking to school with my childhood friends. They had no idea that I was suffering and to be honest, how would they have known? I couldn't tell them. I had learned from a young age to hide the pain from everyone, even from my family. In those days, depression wasn't even on the radar. In most cases if a child misbehaved they were given Ritalin and diagnosed as a "bad child."

I would sit in class and zone out the kids and the world around me. I built a shield around myself, what I called my 'personal zone'. What I mean is, they weren't allowed to get too close. If they got too near, I would let them have it. I started at an early age, to teach myself how to live as two personalities. Looking back now, in doing so, it was more detrimental to myself, simply because I was hiding and running from how I felt. Bottling up my feelings was the same as holding a lit match to a wick of dynamite.

When, at times, I allowed myself to release my built -up emotions, it would cause bouts of aggression, desperation and all out mayhem. Then, when the dust had cleared, it was regrets and, in many cases,

I found myself needing to apologize for my actions. And once again, diving right back into a state of deep depression.

In the book that I have written, I repeat many words, because it is the way I found the road to my happiness. It is important to always repeat these steps. For the better part of my life, I couldn't say most of these words. The first step is telling yourself "I am depressed". In most cases, humans have problems facing the fact that they are not perfect. Let's be honest, none of us are perfect.

In my case, I wish that I had read a book like this. Not written by someone that has only studied the world of depression, but someone like me, who experienced depression first hand. A guy that, most of his life, felt that he had nothing to live for, that he was a burden to his family and wondered if he was dead, would they even shed a tear. I felt like that. I walked in those shoes. Believe me, I am not saying that I am the Messiah that will lead you out of the darkness that lives in your mind. I am telling you my story because, if I can find a way to leave depression and the feeling of hopelessness in the past where it belongs, through my stories and repetitive messages, I feel that you can make your life a happier place. Hopefully, you can find a life that is as fruitful as I have, now that I have changed my surroundings and friends. I found peace within my mind. Even those that don't suffer from depression should read this book, so they too can help someone in their life that suffers from depression. It can give you a better understanding of the illness. Most people have trouble with things they don't understand. I recall, as a child, hearing my parents speaking when they thought I wasn't around. They would argue about which one of them was at fault for the behaviour of their son. At first it made me angry and then very sad. I remember going to my bedroom and putting my head on my pillow and wiping away tears, feeling that their arguments were my fault. Let's be honest, no child should be made to feel like that. When I look at my children now, laughing and playing, it brings incredible joy to me. That's how children should feel, not that he or she is a burden.

Now, I am not in any way blaming my parents. They were immigrants who had very little knowledge of the English language, let alone that their son was depressed. When I was older, I recollect speaking to my parents. They had deep regrets that they weren't there emotionally for me. I reassured them that I never thought that it had been in any way their fault. I wasn't aware, let alone them, that that was the reason for my behavior. It is important for you, as a depressed person to get help. When you suffer, everyone that is part of your life gets dragged in. It may cause, at some time, your loved ones to pick up and leave. The ones that stay are hurting around you, and that is not, in any way, fair to either of you. Although it does take bravery to face yourself and tell yourself or someone else that you are depressed, why would you want to continue feeling hopeless? You need to find the strength and courage to pick yourself up. Life is worth living. The battle will be won.

How can non-sufferers understand what it must feel like to live in the shoes of the depressed? Well I'm going to try and give you three examples, one from my youth, one from my twenty's and one from my forty's, which should give you a good idea. As a youth, it wasn't as though I didn't have good times. That would be a lie. Although there were many happy days, there were just as many sad days. The good days happened when I could hide the darkness inside my mind. I could keep my thoughts of sadness still. They were great. It took a great deal of energy to do this, but darkness was always lurking. You know that at any time it can come rushing back and that's no way to live. When you can no longer hide your depression, you will feel less control. As a child, I remember playing with my friends, losing control and most times regretting it. Thus, I would go weeks going to school and then coming right home and closing my bedroom door, so that I wouldn't hurt anyone. I found peace alone in my own world. There it was safe, with no interaction. Can you imagine how I felt, that by keeping away from other people, my life would be "safe"? How can that be good for your sanity? To live in fear that, at any time, you could lose your self-control. Although I learned to get along with my friends as I got older, it was a constant battle to control my impulses, and not to lose control at times. I felt the strain was so taxing that I would take breaks from my friends and hide, as I had done so many times before in my life. It had always been my safe place, not only for me, but also for anyone that was in my life.

As I approached the end of my teens, I became great at hiding my true self. To others, I had started living as two personalities, the Bammer and Tristan James.

The Bammer was the cool guy that had no fear and Tristan James was depressed and scared of his own shadow. It started to be easier to live as the Bammer and sure, why would I want anyone to know that I had depression? I recall, so many times, looking into the abyss, at times being in a group of people and not even hearing a word of what they were saying. I was, at best, worried and instead of looking forward I was hesitant. I spent most nights trying to plan the next morning and never thought about planning for the future. For me, it was trying to get through every day without feeling that at some point, I would make a "bad" choice. I wished I could have a life like my friends. Life was easy for them but for me, most of my youth, each day was filled with anxiety and worrying about the unknown, the "what if". When I was ready to become a man, I was in a word, terrified and I was concerned that my depression would also control the next chapter of my life.

CHAPTER TWO

THE DAY I TURNED TWENTY WAS twenty days before my first marriage. It would become the worst ten years and some of the most depressed days of my life. I believed that getting married would start a new life, living with my wife and leaving my youth in the rear-view mirror, making everything better. Looking back, I was so wrong. When I was so mentally unstable how could I have believed that, in any way, going from one place to another could change my situation or my mental state? During this time, I gained a lot of weight and the truth of my depression became even more deeply rooted. I now believe that my wife also suffered from depression and when two negatives come together, nothing can be positive. This was the truth for ten years. We tried for years and then we tried having a child to save our marriage. I must say I feel blessed to have had a wonderful child from that marriage, but I also believe that it had been the wrong choice at that time. As a result, my relationship with my child has always been strained. My relationship with his mother created a hostile living environment that was unfair for him. I have always felt that. It has had a long-lasting effect on his mindset. We have always had struggles in our relationship because every day of that relationship, I was just fighting for my sanity. My depression levels had at times been uncontrollable. I became a workaholic, working seven days a week so I had a reason to stay away from home. I started drinking and doing drugs on a regular basis, so I could deal with my depression. I was confused, and I had entertained ending my life more than once. Thanks to some inner strength, I found the courage to leave the marriage, although it had been a tough decision to leave my child behind and start over to rebuild my life. The thought of letting my parents down was very upsetting to me. It was also frightening. The depression levels in my mind had taken a toll on my body. I needed to get out and I did.

CHAPTER THREE

WHEN I TURNED THIRTY, IT WAS THE easiest time for my mind. I was at peace more than at war with my positive mental state. I had found my new wife. I had two more children and I thought that I had beat depression. I found the secret way out and it was behind me. That's when you get caught off guard, just when everything seems to be going well, you don't see it coming. All of a sudden it smashes your world into pieces once again. You are not prepared, in any way, for what is about to happen. I was so ignorant.

I felt that I had kicked depression to the curb for good, and that it would never find its way back to the forefront of my life. Depression is not something that I believe ever leaves the mind. I believe, with knowledge and understanding, you can learn to have complete control over it. I have taught myself that. Although I have had more bad days than good, in the first forty-eight years of my life, the last two have been filled with so much happiness. It's the little things that make life worth living and to be honest I couldn't be more excited to live the next fifty years. I hope that when you read this book and feel the passion that I felt, it will show you that you can live happily.

After you're done reading, start the way I did. Say positive words over and over, until you have no more fear. Do the work, you're worth it, and I promise when you feel positive, the clouds around your heart and mind, will clear and be filled with sun and warmth.

CHAPTER FOUR

THERE ARE MANY MEN AND WOMEN,
that I believe live with depression every day, having
lived and suffered without ever letting anyone know.
They have not even acknowledged to themselves
that they are depressed. It is easier to suffer in their
own mind. You are stealing from yourself! When
you are in a relationship and you hide that you are
depressed, you are stealing from your partner too.
Sooner or later, they will feel your pain. Over time,
it will be detrimental to your relationship. You can't

live in hiding forever and eventually you will break down. When I started letting friends and family know what I was going through, it was a relief to them, as well as to myself. Many of the people in my life told me that they were surprised. Many that had felt my wrath, had always suspected, but had been too afraid of my reaction to tell me. I'll be honest, the feedback was amazing and a bit hard to hear. In some cases, I had made my loved ones afraid, to approach me. I am under the belief that most of us are too afraid to let ourselves be seen as weak, or believe that there is something wrong with our minds. But let's be honest, do you believe that most humans are without faults? When you read about mass shootings and such crimes, the story is always the same, he or she was different. They stayed to themselves. They were outcasts, and people never saw it coming. Or was it just that no one paid attention. Depression takes over your self-control.

Help if you see the signs, don't ignore them, don't judge, and show compassion. Most sufferers only inflict pain on themselves in various ways and in the worst cases they take their own life. I have been there. I was strong enough, luckily, to take a different road. Controlling your depression is the way to a happier life. And you can do it!!

CHAPTER FIVE

THE DEPRESSION THAT I LIVED WITH, was like fighting a war every day. Each moment felt that at any point or any place, I could reach my boiling point. Where most people find it simple to let things slide off their back, I felt, for most of my life, that I have two people that I have been sharing mind and body with. As my growth periods in life would accelerate, I mentally lived as two people, one was born Tristan James and the other, my alter ego, the "Bammer". I am both excited, yet fearful, but I believe that I need to share my story with everyone in the world, most of all my fellow suffers.

I was born to two Italian immigrant parents and had been a happy boy from conception until the age of five. It was at this point, I had my first episode of overwhelming depression and anger. On that occasion, my parents were going out for the evening. Our home, a tiny bungalow, had a small window seat in the front room of the house. I had conveyed my displeasure to my parents, for leaving me for the night, but they told me that, although they understood, they were still leaving and to be a good boy. As my parents got into their car, I watched from the window and experiencing my first real incident of depression and anger, I raised my hand and broke the window. That was the first sign of any escalation of depression. Now, at my age, I understand that I was already living in a depressed state.

I started Junior Kindergarten that same year,

already I had already given my fellow students and teachers, reason to always be on guard around me. Because of my depression, I truly believed that I would continue to be judged by other people and children around me, so I devised a way to always keep people at bay. I figured out, that if I never let anyone get close to me, I would never have to explain the way that I was feeling inside. This, I believe, was the start of my dual personalities as well. I will always remember my first fight with a boy who had simply told me I was quiet, and at that point, how I unleashed my fury. Even as a young boy, I felt convinced that I could control my feelings if I wanted to, so I developed a love for martial arts. My parents believed it would help me deal with my frustrations, but it turned out it was only masking tape. I had found a release for my frustrations in the physical sense, but it did not help me, in any way, to control my mental state. At this point, in my mind, I felt that my parents thought I was a "rotten apple" and I also thought the reason for my parent's constant arguments were my fault. My parents were simple Italian farmers that came to a different country, for a better life, and had neither the patience nor understanding, to help their son in need. I would test my parents at every turn. At times, it felt like chaos to them so, in their ignorance, they began disciplining me physically but to no avail. I would struggle with my parents throughout my adolescent years, engaging in many arguments, resulting in their application of further discipline, which consisted of only one thing, strapping me with a belt. Thinking of it today, how, in any way, can you physically discipline a child to make them understand that violence is not the answer. My mother and I had many discussions, but my mother was a young woman, struggling with two young children and a very unsupportive, older husband. My father was a hard worker who had done what every immigrant had done before and after him. He made certain his family had shelter, food and clothes on their backs, though provided very little parental help and support for my mother, who struggled with the behavior of her son. In those days, the word depression was not common vocabulary. As a child, I resented my mother. I was crying for help, not punishment. I needed her to understand what I was feeling inside, but she would just say to me, that I needed to behave in a proper manner, there was nothing wrong with me, I was just nuts.

Today I now realize that I was tough on my mom who was just a woman who lacked resources and education, never able to truly understand what I was going through and how it was affecting my life. I believe it made it harder for me, impossible to trust my parents so, in my mind my depression continued to grow as I became more isolated.

CHAPTER SIX

THROUGHOUT THE NEXT FEW YEARS of life, my frustration grew. It was recommended that I seek professional help because, at school, the teachers saw that I was consistently growing more frustrated every day. I was sent to the hospital, where they did many tests, including brain scans and a complete body x-ray, to see if the frustration was caused by physical or mental ailments. All the tests concluded that there were no physical ailments of any kind. The school and my parents came to an agreement that I would see a counsellor so, without wanting to, I agreed to see the therapist. As soon as I got into the therapist's office, she started asking me questions that I was completely uncomfortable with, not only questions about me, but also about my family. It felt like she was attacking my mother and father about how they were raising me, and all that did, was put me completely over the edge. I proceeded to destroy her office and after I was done, I was asked to never come back. I remember being at home that night and crying in my room. I had had another breakdown in my depressed state, the most explosive bout of anger to that point in my life.

The next few years I waged an ongoing battle with myself, within my own mind, being so fearful of my actions at that point. It became increasingly hard to get up every day and mingle with people, at home, school or in everyday life. My parents were just more comfortable sweeping it under the rug.

After all, it was much easier for them to never speak about it, to pretend that depression would leave me, then they would never have to deal with it again, that magically I would grow out of it at some point in my life and it would go away. I realized at a young age, that I could not draw support from my parents, so I never shared my feelings with them again.

By the time I was eight years old, the principal and I had become great friends, to the point that the principal made daily jokes that it was Tristan's job to keep me company each day. The principal was a very understanding and compassionate man and, in my heart, I believed he thought I was a good person. Back in those days, mental illness was not really "accepted" as an issue, either through ignorance or lack of knowledge. When you were a "bad child" you simply went to the doctor, who then wrote a prescription for Ritalin, the answer to everything, but that was only more masking tape. It never dealt with my depression. It helped with some of my anger, but it was not the answer. My depressed frame of mind grew darker and I continued to keep everyone away from getting to know me. I was a good student despite my anger and depression, but it was much easier on me to keep to myself. By my eighth year, I had started making a reputation for myself with the other children, I was not to be messed with. It was so much easier to push people away, than it was to tell them how I felt. I felt like I was the only person in the world who was so messed up at such an early age. Even living alone in my own world was such an accomplishment.

I wish today that there were no eight–year-old children feeling the things that I felt every day for years, but I know that isn't the case. The writing of this book is still hard for me, because part of me still feels that even though I can cope with my depression, I worry about letting my guard down, allowing the world to judge and ridicule me. I now have a firm grasp on my depression at this stage in my life, and I am not afraid to let everyone know. I hope that, people will pick up this book, because I feel today that the fear of the unknown can no longer hold me within its death grip.

CHAPTER SEVEN

BY THE TIME I WAS EIGHT YEARS OLD, depression was full steam ahead. Being only a young boy, I could only understand how I felt. I never understood the word depression at that point, had never heard or seen it used anywhere, never understood what was going on inside me. I'm not looking for a pity party. It took a lot of pain and suffering before I reached out for help from the greatest two people in my life, my wife and my Doctor. They have both given me the love, understanding, guidance and the will to never give up, that was necessary to win my fight with depression. Being depressed, living within a depressed emotional state, never truly leaves you, but I have found the internal strength and the will to continuously learn to fight this awful affliction.

Today I appreciate more, that my mother was an incredible woman. She was a hard worker, probably exhausted beyond recognition. All she was doing was trying to be a loving mother to a sick child in need, but in a depressed state you can not find any rhyme or reason for the way you feel. You just know that you are not getting all your mother's attention, and all you can feel is that you are being ignored. It is how depression worked inside me, at times triggering extreme anger, followed by long stretches of violence. Those were long, dark, days for my mind. Fear of the unknown was what I suppose was the most worrisome.

I remember being ten years old and the pain of

everyday life was too much to bear. I was very big for a ten-year old, being around five foot six inches tall and weighing about one hundred and fifty-six pounds and I knew I was stronger than all the kids I grew up with. Many times, I unleashed my extreme anger and fought many battles with anger and violence, feeling like my head would explode because I couldn't understand why it was so hard to control my feelings.

Over the next two years, I was plagued with multiple health issues, that resulted in many trips to the hospital for treatment. By the time I was twelve, I had transgressed into an even deeper depressive state. I had made a real name for myself as a tough guy, a street fighter and this was when I received the nickname "Bammer". I remember the first time I was arrested, a week before my thirteenth birthday. I had gone out to get my dad a pack of cigarettes at the local corner store and ran into a bad situation. Someone tried to steal the money for my dad's cigarettes from me. Most normal youth of that age would have run away, but not me. To this day, I don't have a detailed recollection of what happened, I must have blacked out. I just remember my friends being there, they couldn't believe what had happened. This was my first experience blacking out and having no recall or memory of the situation. I had lost control and knew that I was in a bad emotional state. I understood I needed to better restrain my mood swings to be able to keep myself under control, and that it would be a long road ahead. That was the day the "Bammer" was born, becoming the person that I would mold my life around. What I mean by this is, that it was much easier to live as the "Bammer," someone who was much friendlier and more personable. It wasn't like I was unaware I was still Tristan James, but when I looked in the mirror and saw Tristan, I was not happy. It was much easier to take on the alter ego the "Bammer" so for the rest of my life, I lived as "Bammer," putting Tristan away, so that no one would discover the real me. The person that everyone knew, was the "Bammer." For me, it became my way of life.

By the time I was twelve years old, I was six foot one inch tall and about two hundred pounds. I remember the teachers would always be on guard. But there was one teacher, Jim White, who was a real fun-loving teacher. I wish he could have taught my children. He was a tough nosed Irishman, a take no bullshit kind of guy. He was very instrumental in my development, by using his knowledge, his recognition of my athletic ability and telling me he knew I was a good kid. He helped direct my strength and size into something positive, turning me on to the world of sports. I played hockey as a tough nosed defenseman, but my true love was the game of football. I was good at it, having many recruiters, from many colleges, asking me to play for them. It had been a pivotal point in my life, a time when I was able to leave my anger on the field, a very positive feeling for me. I guess the impact of the full body contact was an avenue for my anger to be expelled, but maybe the guys I played against would feel differently, much differently. Playing football and hockey were great avenues, but I still could not escape the depressed state of my mind that was always there.

The depression and what I was going through, I believe, should have been recognized as an illness. Depression, at its core, makes you feel that you are not worthy. Most experts in the field of mental illness, believe that treatment using antidepressants or other medications can subdue or control the imbalance of emotions in the brain that leads to the state of depression. I, myself, have been on many brands of antidepressants and although, from time to time, they helped me deal with everyday life, it is, at best, just another band aid solution. Unfortunately, medication only subdues the feelings, but cannot change the fact that people in a state of depression, have brains that are wired in ways in which there is no irreversible solution. I have lived this way for such a long time I know, that only by dealing with your depression continuously, can you control the affects and the many stages of depression. It can only be treated, first and foremost, after admitting to yourself that you need help. Today there are many more sites, books, and professionals dealing with the battle against depression, however I feel that the severity of this illness is still not completely understood. Personally, I have done studies, talked to many people about depression, and found that very few have sought help. The conclusion I have come to, is that you need to release your depression and anxiety on a day to day basis. Remember you are not in this fight alone!

I believe we have made great strides, however, I believe that people experiencing depression are still fearful of the negative opinions and comments, the stigma of mental illness by people who do not understand. Most people's reactions are to diminish depression as a less serious affliction, or to not deal with it at all. It's time to take living in a depressed state as serious as any other medical condition. In my opinion, depression should be considered a disease, not only an illness.

CHAPTER EIGHT

I TRULY BELIEVE THAT DEPRESSION AND people who live in a depressed state can be cured, but first, they must truly accept their condition. It is not something that can be cured by medicine and thinking that medicine alone can fix the root of the problem, is not the solution. You must come to the realization that you need help to find solutions that provide happiness in your day to day life, so that there are no destructive moments of inertia. In my many discussions with people in the past, who have been open about their depression, some feel the only true cure is to end their lives. Therefore, I believe it is urgent that you look around, and notice the people that are showing signs of depression. You may be their last chance! You could talk to them about getting the help they need to save their life. In my life, there have been more dark days, than days where my light has been bright. I have had to cope with feeling that, at times, I was a burden to my parents, feeling like I was carrying the weight of all the world on my back. I spent many days in bed, lacking the energy to even go to the washroom. That was what depression did to me, it sucked the energy out of everything I did. Imagine, that you have handcuffs and shackles on, that anytime you moved they followed and restricted your every movement. That's the way it has been most of my life. The pain to just do everyday things was, at times, unbearable. That is what living in a depressed state of mind feels like, you are a prisoner in your body and mind. To truly understand, the way I felt for most of my life, you would have to imagine walking alone. I could see that I was not alone, so it felt like blocking out the people around me would be much easier to deal with, than to let them look at me and see that I was in pain. I felt this pain would be seen as a sign of utter weakness. Some days, I would jump in my car, driving forever with no specific destination, just playing sad songs. That is the worst thing one can do to themselves. Imagine being on a diet and someone drops a donut on your desk. Not nice! The same goes for someone that is suffering from depression. But that's what I did so many times in my life. I never knew where I was going, but I drove until I could cope with the state my mind was in, at that moment. It was the way I dealt with depression in my early and late twenty's. I felt as though I had no one to talk to and was not ready to share my feelings. I was living in a depressed state and it was easier to keep Tristan in the back of my mind then to deal with it, letting the "Bammer" carry on in my mind was easier. He didn't have as hard a time dealing with life, but by having two personalities, it allowed the depression to rise to dangerous levels and at its highest point it would be catastrophic. And that's where so many fears in my mind lead to, the feeling that one day I might cause harm to myself or to the loved ones around me. I always felt the need to keep moving or talking, to keep occupied, otherwise my mind would slow down and then I would feel my depression at the farthest, darkest place in my mind. At times, I would work eighteen-hour days for months on end, feeling like I was running away from the evil man in my brain. The problem is, you can't run from yourself, it's too exhausting. I felt so depressed, I was worse off when I was running. It's a viscous cycle that would always start, stop, and repeat. It was at the height of all this, that I found new ways to deal with my life in a depressed state.

CHAPTER NINE

I WAS ALWAYS AFRAID OF THE WAY MY

mind was full of emotions, but I was more afraid to

share or deal with any of it, as a youth, a teenager

or an adult. I was still, on the surface, able to find

success in my business life, a strength that I inherited

from my mother. What I mean is, my mother and

I both lived in the depressed state of mind. We had

been able to find the strength to forge on, a strength

we both possessed, allowing us to find a way to

succeed financially. But make no mistake about it,

it was just masking the way I saw life. I had been looking through tinted windows that, even though I had success in finances and in business, was the only success that I felt I had, until I met my wife. I spent most days feeling very unhappy, looking at myself in the mirror and hating the man I saw, thinking, why couldn't I be happy? At times, I felt like throwing in the towel. When I met the woman, who would become my wife, it was maybe the first time I felt alive, but I did not share with her that I had depression and how I lived most days of my life in darkness. When I met my wife to be, it did bring my depression levels to the lowest they had been in my life. She was young and beautiful combined with her warmth and loving ways, made this an easier time. This is what depression levels are like, having the highest of highs, to what I call the moment of inertia, my living, waking, fear of the impending deepest and lowest of lows. It occurs when all your stored-up anger and aggressions release at once, so understanding your depression levels can limit the fear of living in chaos. I spent many years trying to figure things out and although I'm not a doctor or therapist, I am a deeply depressed man that has taught himself to deal with the levels within my mind. There is no cure for the way depression lives in the brain, but I have talked to many people, explaining my theory and have seen the change, not only in myself, but in the people, that have tried my methods. It is my hope that all sufferers deal with their depression, because there is a better life out there. Unfortunately, it was a long road to understand my feelings, having depression as an unwanted enemy in my mind for so many years.

I witnessed many friends and family suffer in silence and I couldn't do a thing about it. I, myself, was walking in their shoes. I will share some of their stories, but I will not be using their true names.

Having personally dealt with the way depression made a home in my head, I am no longer afraid; in a way, I feel it is therapeutic. If someone feels the need to pass judgement on me, that is their choice but, believe me, it doesn't make me depressed anymore, because these days I feel great in my own shoes. Although every day can be filled with struggles, I am in control of my life and how I handle my depression.

CHAPTER TEN

THIS IS THE STORY OF MY BEST FRIEND MT. Although he has passed, he will always live on in my heart and I miss him so much. I met Mr. MT when I was about thirty-five. We couldn't have been more opposite, but we just found friendship in what we both loved, things like coffee, smoking and most of all golf. He may have been the worst golfer the world has ever seen, but it didn't matter, he loved the game more than anyone. It was where he and I were most at peace in our minds, away from the world around us. We would spend every weekend together on the golf course, where we talked about everything. I felt so blessed that this man and I spent so many moments together, and those became some of the best days of my life. We were both, in many ways, pillars or rocks, helping each other in ways that most people would be lucky to find in their life. In the years that followed, we shared our life stories, and found out that we were both suffering from living in a constant state of depression. I feel that was why I became so interested in understanding what depression was, to understand how and why depression lived inside me and others, by better educating myself. I believed if I could understand the inner workings of my mind, then maybe I could find peace and live a better life than I had up to then. Mr. MT told me he believed that he also had been living with deep depression all his life, using drugs and alcohol as the way he would deal with his emotional highs and lows. He had been married, but his wife could not deal with his addictions and one day after work, he went home, opened a beer and then, realizing that he was home alone, noticed a letter on the kitchen table. It said "I've tried to understand you, but you have never accepted that you need help and I can't live here any longer." She had then left and taken their young child, resulting in him becoming even more depressed. I believed he would always live in that depressed state of mind, although, he had told me, that the time we spent together were the best years of his life. I do know that he never lived life to the fullest, and I only wish that I could have given him ten years of my life. I believe that with more time and love, he would have died happier, but God has everyone on his clock, and even though I find it hard to believe, that at the age of forty-nine, it was his time. I felt that he gave me so many years of true friendship and that's how I will always remember him, a true buddy. Although it's easier for me to be positive, it has taken many years to heal my heart following his passing, and I still think of him every day.

Today, I have taught myself to keep my depression at what I call manageable levels, my key to success, and I believe that I can help all of you. When Mr. MT passed away, I was once again at what I call the danger level of my depressed state, where I could not control my anger or keep my focus on day to day life. It was another reminder, that I still had no idea when my depression would escalate, and once again rise to the highest and most dangerous level. I was like a child watching a scary movie, who can't stop watching, even though they know they should.

The next year of my life after MT passed, I didn't deal with how I was feeling inside my mind. His death was sudden and I felt that I had so much left to say. From his diagnosis with cancer, to the time of his passing, was only three months. He had reassured me that he was in good shape and that he would beat it, he told me that I was worrying for nothing, that we would soon be on the links. I remember his last day, being at his side, the ghost of the man he once was, and when I was talking to him, it was so hard. The day he died, I felt that a piece of my heart died with him.

CHAPTER ELEVEN

ONCE AGAIN I WALKED AROUND DAY to day, lost in my mind. I was short tempered, not having time for anyone or anything, and the cause of pain to my wife and kids. In my mind, I just felt that I was staying out of the way, but my kids were telling their mom that their dad was ignoring them. My wife tried to explain that I was just sad and it was true, I was truly suffering. It had been the first time in my life that someone I loved like a brother, was ripped out of my life. I felt so angry with God and even wondered how a God that loves us, could take the man I called my brother. It was getting harder to keep control, once again feeling I was losing my mind. This event would begin my first step towards seeking help, and so, with my wife's support and the love of my family, I reached out for help from the man I now call my second father, my doctor, Dr. MH. I always felt like I was alone as a child, but through my many talks with my doctor and, with my wife's guidance, I once again started to work through my hardest days since the passing of MT. Depression comes in waves. At times, you feel in control, but until you understand your levels of depression, and what triggers you, it can always return. I knew that even though I was in a better state of mind, I was fooling myself thinking that I could control depression from happening again. I was always on edge and still not happy because, deep down inside, I felt that I was a ticking time bomb, having felt this way for most of my life. I had lived as two people, outward, as the "Bammer", I appeared strong and didn't fear anything, but in my mind, as Tristan, I was so scared of who and what I was. I was living as a prisoner of my mind, and having these two personalities was the only way I knew how to cope since I was twelve years old.

CHAPTER TWELVE

IMAGINE WHEN YOU LOOK IN THE mirror you see two faces and you hate them both. The "Bammer" was easier to look at, he was after all, what I wanted people to see. As the "Bammer", I didn't have to share that I was a man who lived life afraid to let anyone know that inside my head was confusion. I felt that when MT died, all the work I had put in, had once again regressed. I could fall back into my depressed world, but that wasn't how I wanted to feel. Let's face it, fear is what keeps most of us from true success, always keeping us at bay. Fear is the single most misunderstood word in my opinion. In business, I was fearless, because I felt that hard work over fear would always win out, but happiness through financial gains is not the key to true and lasting joy. I would find out, much later in my life, that although the purchase of material objects like homes and cars would make me happy in the short term, they hardly got a chance to collect dust before I forgot about them, having little meaning in the long run. I always found myself moving my body faster than my mind. Throughout my life I tried to make my father proud and he would remind me, nothing can give you peace until you find what you need; that's true happiness. I used to look at him and think, what hell are you talking about? I fooled myself into believing I was happy, but he knew me better than I knew myself. I have the most nonjudgmental father, a man who came from nothing and made a good life for himself and our family. I understood then, that my father had figured out what his life was truly about. He told me that I would figure it out one day and never made me feel bad about the way I lived my life, always being there for me. Today, as a father, I can only imagine how hard it must have been for my father, to see all the struggles I had faced in my life. I thought he was unaware when, all along, he was truly waiting for me to share with him, how I was feeling. Now I wish that I had let him know. I couldn't admit it to myself, I was so confused, let alone share it with him. I was carrying the guilt for all the pain that I caused, to the people in my life. I felt that if I just kept all the feelings that were causing me confusion, bottled up inside to myself, one day, with age, they would just disappear. What a fool I was, for so long. My father never pried. When I look back today, at all the times that I felt I disappointed in him, that if I only had

had the courage to speak about those feelings, it would have been a much easier and more fulfilling life. I am happy that I have found my voice and now have a grip on how to deal with my depressed state. I have the most love for the man I am proud and honored to call my father.

CHAPTER THIRTEEN

WHEN MY MOTHER PASSED, IT WAS the worst and most self-destructive time in my life. My mother was, in a word, wonderful, but as tough as nails. I remember so many times I must have made my mother's life hell on Earth, but no matter what, she loved me. I love and miss her dearly. I can remember receiving the call that she had passed and for the first time in my depressed life, I openly wept for the entire night. I have no regrets, having had a wonderful relationship with my mother. Some days I feel she is talking to me and no, I am not nuts, just hopeful. I feel that I made my mother's life very difficult when my mother was alive, calling her every night on my way home, her asking me if everything was alright, me of course always saying yes, but she knew it was not true. I didn't need her to feel my pain. A mother's understanding of their children is far better than we think, she knew, and always reminded me that moms know when things aren't right. I smile when I think of how she would say "I know you son." I miss her so much today, the thought of her makes me happy, but for eight months after her death, it tore out my soul. When my mother passed, I retired, because I could. I wanted to be there for my father, but my depression was at a dangerously high level at that time, having not only lost my best friend, but then my mother. For many years before losing both, I was happy most days, but when I lost my mother, I fell hard. I didn't see that I was heading down a spiraling road, hard and fast, in the worst possible way. Within a few months, I left my wife, began taking drugs, drinking excessive amounts of alcohol and partying like I was eighteen, with only two hours of sleep a night. This behaviour went on for months, even sleeping with other women I didn't even care about. In my mind, I was living like a king, spending outrageous amounts of money, completely and totally out of my mind. I remember getting up one morning, driving the new Camaro that I had bought, across Canada to Vancouver having friends there, spending a solid month partying, doing drugs, drinking alcohol and many other things that I am now embarrassed to even talk about. After a month, I drove back for forty-eight straight hours and that's when I hit the wall. Following two nights at home, I was hospitalized and discovered that it was not just dehydration, I was sick. I was diagnosed with diabetes, my sugar levels being 27.9. I realized that could have been the end of my life, and sitting in the hospital bed, I knew that I didn't want to live this way anymore. Thinking about how fast my depression was making me destroy my life with my own hands, I decided I needed help. This is not the way I would have wanted my mother to see me. Taking the next six months to return to normal health, I knew that I didn't want to ignore my depression again, that I needed to deal with it and not just with medication. I needed to understand what the root of the problem was, and hence, the reason for my depression. I discovered that I could change the patterns in my mind that gave me those dangerous highs and the extreme lows, and I made it my mission to live a more balanced life. Although my mother was always there for me, I knew that she too had suffered from bouts of depression. She wished that she would have gotten help for me. It has made me understand that I must help myself and anyone who asks me for help, because, allowing yourself to feel that you are alone in the world of depression, is wrong. I believe that while most people suffer alone in their world, like my mother and myself, it is not the way one should live. Seeking help and letting your feelings be known, will allow you to start to see the light at the end of the tunnel. I wish I could have found it myself, instead of feeling so ashamed that I'd rather keep it to myself. I hope my mother is happy in her new life with God.

CHAPTER FOURTEEN

ANOTHER STORY I WOULD LIKE TO share is that of another dear friend who I will, for his privacy, call Mr. Y. When I told him that I was writing this book about depression, for the first time in our friendship, he told me that he too has lived with depression. He was surprised that I was a depressed person. I told him that this was the main reason I'm letting people know, because people living with depression are not always transparent. I believe that this is the unfortunate reality in most cases. If my story can make someone else feel comfortable to talk about it, then I have succeeded. We talked mostly about how, like myself, he felt ashamed, embarrassed at opening up to being ridiculed and I knew where he was coming from. I explained that if depression was a human, it would be a bully, and when that bully was around, you would run, hide and stay hidden. That's what a depressed state is and at its highest levels, it can turn into acts of violence in some people, who feel like that is their only alternative. That's the danger of staying in a depressed state for too long, it's like air in a balloon within your mind, too much air and it will eventually burst. At times Mr. Y was not getting my theories, but the more times I explained my theories to him, the more he understood them. I'm glad to say, that he has put my explanations into effect in his everyday life, and I couldn't feel happier. He asked me where I learned all my theories and how I obtained them. I explained to him, like I tell anyone reading or talking to me about my research theories, they are theories that I devised for use in everyday life and I have no problem saying I'm not in any way a therapist or doctor. They work for me, so I just figured they may work for others as well. I have tried these theories on myself and on friends that suffer from depression, and have seen a transformation. I feel that living in a depressed state for ninety percent of my life, gives me, in my opinion, a very good understanding of how depression works. I have written this book for the sole purpose of trying, with all my heart and soul, to let people know that I understand how they feel, having personally lived in their shoes. I'm not looking to my peers for their approval in any way. I just want to help someone in need, to let people know, that even those who do not want others to know that they suffer, can read this book and find the courage to help themselves. You must find the strength inside you, find what we all deserve; true happiness. I have not felt more alive in my whole life and don't care that I put my life story out there. I'm not going to live in my mind alone. I have found through my studies, research and living with depression, that it helps to share the information. I now feel free and my soul is alive. I chose to understand, not only how depression works, but I feel comfortable telling anyone who can understand my message. They themselves can compare the similarities of my life to their own. Those who don't want to let depression rule their minds and want to deal with their depressive state, will start fighting back.

CHAPTER FIFTEEN

MY NEW AND WONDERFUL BEST friend, Mr. MF, will always have a piece of my heart. I learned that our hearts can always find room for more and MF is, in a word, electrifying. What I mean is, he could brighten a room with just his contagious smile. If you want to be miserable, I dare you to with MF around. MF has also lived a good part of his life in a depressed state, but, his presence still fills a room with light. Life is funny, as our friendship grew it was amazing how much we had in common, the day to day struggles and the way he also found it easier to let people see his alter ego. It was so easy to talk about everything with him. We met at comedy school and instantly hit it off, like we had been friends all our lives. Although we were so different, we were also similar in numerous ways and it was so easy for both of us to talk about our lives. I had not felt a true friendship with anyone since Mr. MT passed and although no friendship is the same, the bond was so similar, that I felt that Mr. MT was guiding it from above. After many hours of conversation, I asked MF what he would think if I shared my struggles, my courage and the way I had finally chosen to achieve a better life. In sharing my story, I felt I was better able to understand my depression, how it had affected not only my life, but also the lives of so many around me. I remember he was not only supportive, he loved the idea. I had found the will to stand up to depression, by recognizing that I was depressed. It took courage to teach myself how to deal with it and it's still a constant struggle in my life. I knew that if someone suffering like myself, was supporting me and believed in my findings, it would give me the strength to put it out there. The thought of being judged was so scary, however, I felt that if I was able to help someone out there, by publishing this book, then any judgment I faced would be worth it. MF has been the most supportive friend. With his friendship, no matter what I feel or how tough my day has been, he always finds the right words to pick up my spirits. I feel that I have been doing the same for him as well. All our time together is not spent talking about depression but if I'm down, he always helps me see the light. It's so important to have a friend that is a positive role model. MF has said many times, how positivity can't find you if you are around negative people, misery loves company. I find spending my time with people who are positive, even when life kicks your ass, helps to keep me going. You need to find the light at the end of the tunnel and hold on tight through the dark days, and soon the darkness will give up on you. MF is the embodiment of that premise. He can bring sunlight to the darkest of storms, just being around a man like him can make you smile and it is wonderful. I find it so hard to believe that this man could have ever had a day of depression, showing me, that there are ways, that we, as sufferers of depression, can control our state of mind. I can say it because I have lived it. MF himself said that he found every day of his life a battle. Finding the strength to conquer a depressed mind is possible, I truly believe we must, not only for ourselves but for anyone that loves us. There is someone out there that can give you what you need, a counsellor, doctor or therapist, and you deserve it, you just need to believe in them and yourself. MF you have been a God send. You have reaffirmed that

I have so much to be thankful for, been like a brother who was always there for me, listening and laughing. I know that you feel the same. I just want to thank you for being my friend.

CHAPTER SIXTEEN

I REMEMBER AFTER I GOT HOME, I started to return to good health, having put the worst time behind me, both mentally and physically. I was sitting, watching television and thinking to myself, I know I have a mental illness and then I stopped blaming it on myself. I make no excuses for all the hurt I caused to myself and all my loved ones, but wasn't satisfied just saying, well this is how my brain is wired, sorry but it's not my fault. I had to find out why or how this happened and how I could prevent it from happening again. How was I going to get the knowledge that I needed to control these feelings in my mind? I knew I wasn't going to just accept that I had no control over my actions and understanding that it was a chemical imbalance of the brain wasn't good enough for me. I wanted to find out why. Theories alone were not enough, accepting that I should tell myself I had mental illness was not enough, so in theory, not accepting that there would be times when I would have no control over the situation. I needed to understand why, at times, my feelings of depression would build to the point that I would become self -destructive. I felt that before I could control my depression, I needed to first study myself. I'm not a doctor or therapist, never studied the inner workings of the brain. I was a caterer, football player, and golfer. Ask me about any of those things and I can give you great explanations, but I know they are not going to give me the answers I was looking for. To be honest, I had no idea, so I simply went to see my doctor.

I asked him if he thought that pills alone would stop depression at the core, already knowing the answer. He told me antidepressants would help, but it would take understanding and time. He asked if I would talk to a therapist and I agreed.

I believe the therapist was great. He listened and gave me good advice, but I was looking for more. Yes, antidepressants helped, but for me they didn't help get the answers that I felt were vital for success. It felt good that, for once in my life, I could talk freely about my depression without feeling ashamed. Some talking works and the medicines help, but for me, they were not good enough. I had done both in the past but, over time, my depression would return and I knew now that it was always a possibility that it could reappear over and over again. Therefore, I was going to be ready by amassing knowledge of the inner workings of my depression. In the past, I had always been too arrogant and ignorant, so I made it my mission to educate myself and my passion to understand how the brain works. I was going to create a theory, an army so to speak, to battle the depressed state of my mind. I was not afraid. I wasn't doing this to write this book. I was ensuring that the reason I had, at times, thought I was going to end my life, would be stopped in its tracks. I knew I had lived with mental illness all my life, but if I could understand why, then I could learn to control it. I wasn't going to wait around for the depression to drag me through the mud any more.

CHAPTER SEVENTEEN

MY STARTING POINT WAS TO MEND my relationship with my wife and my family. I shared with my wife that I had accepted my depression, that I had been living in fear, something she had known for many years. I told her that I wasn't very comfortable talking about the way I felt, but I needed to understand the reason behind my depression. She was happy that I was ready to understand this illness, that it was no longer enough to just say "well okay, I'll try my best not to keep it to myself". That hadn't worked in the past and it wasn't going to work now, so we talked about where to commence my learning, my wife suggesting that I start at the beginning, by reading books and watching videos. They were helpful and well written, but most of things I read or listened to I already knew about. The information was too general, things like, depression was a form of mental illness and a chemical imbalance. This was true, but it wasn't enough. it's not just the thoughts of wonderful memories and being happy, it's about why, in many instances, are there manic levels of depression. I needed to understand why I had spent so many hours watching television and reading. I realized that although depression, in theory, affects everyone differently at times, emotions are like DNA, unique to each person. Each book or lecture increased various aspects of my overall knowledge, but I still felt the need for more information. That's the moment I truly decided to make this the most important work of my life, first for my benefit and then for my friends and family. The next time I sat in my office, I thought back in time and made notes of when my first episode started, wanting to keep it fresh in my mind. I needed to see it on paper, so I started writing about when I was five years old, the first time I had shown signs of depression. It was the beginning of what I felt was the real understanding of my inner-feelings. It felt amazing, not only to see it, but to finally accept it. It was painful to pull out those bad memories, but It was essential, in order to get to where I wanted to go. I needed answers to my questions, so I kept writing about all the times I had acted out and by the time I got to the age of eight, I had about fifteen pages. At this point I started to feel as if a weight was being lifted off my soul and my mind wasn't in such a rush. The more I remembered each incident, the more I was finding out there were so many different levels of depression. While I was thinking about what those levels were, I determined what emotional conditions depression relies on and I was finding this more and more interesting. Sometimes we are not sure what roads we are taking to get our answers, but that's half the fun. I kept going with my notes and remembered how, in the past, I wouldn't let depression out and then I would have major bouts of rage. Other times, like when a friend didn't want to play a game, I was angry for a second, then realizing my anger, it would be easy to regain control. As I chronicled all the highs and lows, I started to see that my depression would not only control my bouts of sadness, it would also lead to emotions of anger and anxiety. Every emotion was, in some way, controlled by the levels of my depression and at this point I was intoxicated seeing it all coming together. I ended up recording the first 30 years of life living in a depressed state, never having previously understood what set off the triggers that released my depression, but as I got to the last few years, I finally understood and got my answers.

CHAPTER EIGHTEEN

I UNDERSTOOD WHAT I HAD LEARNED

and It was the most exited I had been in my life. It was now clear in my mind that I was ready to explain things to MF and my wife. By the time I finished writing down the how, why and when my depression would come and go like waves at the beach, I determined depression had forever been a core part of my life. It worked at being the engine, driving every feeling; anger, love, sadness, and compassion. Although I couldn't always control my emotions, I now believe that for most depression sufferers, it can be harvested. Once again, these are my findings and my theories and I am sharing them with anyone who wants to listen. I'm not in any way saying that I have a doctorate on the subject, but I have lived first hand with depression for 50 years and despite that hardship, I have experienced happiness in my life for the last 2 years. I know that depression cannot be eliminated, but it can be controlled, I am living proof, the Guinea pig for all my research and experiments. How can anyone know depression better than those who suffer from it? In my opinion, I haven't felt more alive and free, so that's why I believe in what I'm sharing with you. No one can make you feel better if you aren't ready to start. I found that in every good or bad time, I had had no control over how long I would allow the levels of my depression to rise. The higher the levels of emotion would travel on its journey to the boiling point, the more the destruction and chaos rose. It was during that chaos that I caused harm to myself and to others, and that's why I needed to find ways to control these levels of depression from rising to where they could be so harmful. I believe this is where so many people carry out their anger and not only harm themselves, but harm everyone around them. Depression is not a free ticket to carry around for your actions in any way. It's why I feel that it is so important that you, as a sufferer of depression, get help. You don't have to keep it locked up in your mind, as I know I did. I wish I had been stronger then, but I am today. You can do it. Stand up, make every day a day without depression. I know it's the way we're wired, but don't be a jackass. It's important to find help, no one is perfect; only fools believe that they are. In this world, you may be surprised to learn that the person you think has it all together, is just like you. At times, I still see people sitting around and I see the pain they are feeling. Before, I wouldn't think twice, I didn't notice that my life was in that same state; you know the old saying 'ignorance is bliss '. As foolish as it was, at times I couldn't even be bothered to stop and ask my friends if they were okay. I felt that if I didn't ask, I wouldn't have to be involved in or have to deal with, someone else's problems. If they said no I'm not, I'm depressed, then I would know they were. I was the guy that didn't want to know, because I was in those same shoes. Maybe I wasn't comfortable that, in return, they may want to know if I was okay. Looking back, I think I was afraid to ask anyone, because maybe they would look at me and think, wow, this 6' 3 280 lb guy knows how I feel because he's depressed too. Food for thought. Although I had lived most of my life in what I call the depressed state of mind, the more I study my feelings and talked to myself, the easier it became to understand that depression is a mental illness. At its core, I was finding that the mind is incredibly hard to understand. It was so amazing to learn that we are all different, that even professionals still don't understand how the mind works. There are studies that explain that most of us only use a small percentage of our brain, and while so many great strides continue to be made, we still can't comprehend all the inner working of the brain. I wish I would have studied that and not catering. Lol. Over the past forty years, we've seen an explosion of technology in many aspects of our life. What we haven't seen is much advancement in the diagnosis of depression and the application of related medications. I feel that for the most part, though there is more awareness, we need to eliminate the stigma of depression, make the sufferers of depression more comfortable that it's okay to be depressed, but it's not okay to suffer alone. Not seeking help simply means staying depressed. The worst thing you can do, is let the feeling grow, because that's how depression can accelerate and get out of control. I remember how I felt most days, and maybe you lived this way yourself. For me, it started at such a young age, I felt confusion about why I was so unhappy. I hated to go to school and would let everyone around me see it and feel it. Then, going home, when most kids where smiling and hugging their parents, I would be mad and barely say anything or even look at my parents. When I got home I would go to my room and just lay on my bed for hours, and when I think about it now, I don't remember having any thoughts at all. And when most kids would play in the park laughing, screaming and smiling, I would just sit on the park bench and stare at the sky. I know that my parents thought they had an anti social child and I know they had no idea that I was crying out for them to just ask me if I was okay. Instead, for them, I believe it was much easier thinking that their young son would one day come out of this and be fine. Simply brushing it under the rug will not help. If you feel that you see any signs that your child is depressed, ask. Don't be afraid to learn that they are feeling funny inside, because most kids don't know they're depressed. You may have a child that is having a hard time understanding that what they are feeling is, at best, confusion, but if they share it with you, you can help. I wish my parents would have said, Tristan, it's okay to tell us how you're feeling; that they wouldn't judge me, but really try to help, and if they couldn't, they would be there by my side. Together we could have taken steps to do whatever was necessary to make me feel better. Unfortunately, most children feel that it's better to deal with these feelings on their own and I know from my own dealings, that it's too much for any child to bear. I lived it and felt so alone. I dealt with it through anger, confusion and many lonely nights. Remembering those long, tough nights alone, feeling that I was never going to let anyone get close enough; not my parents, loved ones or friends, because if I had, they would know I was strange. It's crazy that I thought I could fool anyone, yet I did fool them.

CHAPTER NINTEEN

I REMEMBERED THAT, AS THE YEARS passed, the time when I was 12 and the next violent outburst of my depression found its way out; it got me arrested. I still would never tell anyone that I was so depressed, that I just wanted to cry. To be honest, the longer and the older you get without dealing with depression, the more often you will lose control and that was when I had started to live my dual persona, Tristan was who I truly was, but the Bammer was the guy everyone knew. It had been easier, in my mind, to keep it that way. In hind-sight that was the worst way possible. The more time I spent writing down information from the studies that I read, watched and listened to, I found that, not only was I learning and educating myself, the more I was looking deeper at how my levels of depression varied at times through my life. I could remember at what points I could have slowed down the movement of what I call the ruler levels. Let's say that the digits go from 0 to 100. Using this guide, I could understand at what point control was manageable and where control was not possible. I figured that if I could teach myself how to stay at the bottom of the ruler, depression would stay at a manageable, controlled level, become the base where all emotions are in control. I had discovered a way to make life easier to deal with, but I wasn't satisfied. I not only needed to recall every tough time, but also when there were easier times, to arm myself with the knowledge necessary to visualize levels of controlled depression and out of control depression. If I made notes of every memory, of all the levels of my depressed state, to ensure I would be right about all my findings, I would still be writing this book, so I'll break it down so that I can get done in this millennium. I noted that, when I had found the strength to deal with my depression at the beginning of a situation, there was very little fall out, but when I let it fester my anger and confusion were at their most and their worst. I needed to replay all the memories and situations from my past; to find the secret to my successes dealing with depressed life. That was and will be what I would do, until I felt I could find peace.

When I was finally at the point where I felt, I had all my data and identified all the moments my depression was at the highest levels and at their lowest, I was ready to study the research I had done on all my struggles. I needed to understand why was I able to, at times, stop the escalation and at times, not find the balance. It was frustrating, so I compared, at all ages, the stages of depression in the same range, and noting the times I would be able to stop myself and slow the actions while, at other times, have no control. So, when I closed my eyes in my office, it felt like I was hydroplaning over the play by play of all the memories of every part of my life. I noticed depression at every stage of my life from the age of five, the worst and most destructive times of my life, as if I was watching a movie "The Life of Tristan James"; a life that had no snacks or popcorn. The "movie" of Tristan James felt real, necessary and painful, because I was so deep in thought that I only found the truth. It was so amazing having the strength to look at my life and not be afraid of truly seeing the real me, while feeling all the pain that I had lived with for so long. For about a week, I spent all day playing the movie of my life in my mind, just watching my life unfold. It was very taxing, but at the same time it was what I needed. All my life I had felt like I was running, never wanting to talk about my feelings. I had been more afraid to live, at times wanting death and it still brings a tear to my eye so, as I watched the "movie", it became like it was someone else's life and not mine. It sounds crazy, but I'm telling you as my eyes were closed, I was watching this guy's life, at the same time thinking why doesn't he get help. No shit Sherlock.

Although it was eye opening, I found myself seeing where and when trigger points were switched on and off. As I was floating in the air above, I saw this boy become a young man, wanting to go and help, but I couldn't. I wanted to yell at him like stop, think, no, stop, you need to get help and at those times I would open my eyes, jot down some notes and take a break. It was so hard to exert all that energy and at times I wanted to stop doing it. I lived it all once before, so now, to be able to configure it into this form, was real. It had truly happened and I made myself see, with no fear, the real control of my life, that I had been hurting for so long in this depressive state, I needed to see the "movie" to the end. I studied and watched every manic state, every self-loathing, every fear and every confusion and I started to find out when, and how, I was feeling. I was spotting the situations even before the guy in the movie was, very handsome guy lol. That guy would find instances when he had good times, when he would jump in his car and listen to music and drive and drive, when he just kept going. Then he would turn around, go home and lay in bed in a state of fear, not once letting himself share his depressed feelings. Watching, at times I felt that my heart was going to stop. Wow! Why did this guy not see that he needed help?

When I watched the movie through the years

between the ages of 5 and 34, it was at times hard to see. The truth be told, to truly understand, I needed to see things through my new eyes. I wasn't afraid, but my emotions were being put to the test. It was also the "movie" I had to see for the first time. I was aware that it was my life I was watching but, in the state I had been in, it was like seeing things for the first time. I was looking at what I was hiding from and it was myself; everyone that knew me, not the "Bammer", but Tristan James. It was tiring and mentally exhausting. This was the first steps in the study of my life with depression, where emotions were not running at all levels. Now, I saw how the next eight years of my life had been at the best and lowest levels of depression. During those years, I got married and had more children. When Mr. MT and I were golfing, I found that my mind was still, it wasn't running a race to nowhere, and home life, family life was good. During this time, my levels were easier to control, not because I thought that my depression was gone, but because nothing was causing any dangerous levels. When I had days of depression, I could keep them at bay. At this point, in the "movie" floating around in my mind, I thought, this guy, he's got it all and that's when arrogance finds you. You're not standing on guard and what I mean is, that you let your guard fall. It's when you feel magical, like you have no more depression. Wrong! Although it was becoming boring to watch this part of the "movie" of my life, it was soon getting to the part that was going to get more action than my life could handle. Buckle up! I was now forty-two years old and the last eight years had been filled with more days with very low levels of depression. Soon they would be the highest, most depressed days, that I would ever experience. They would become the darkest and most destructive days as, for the first time in my life, I would have to deal with the death of a best friend. I was blind-sided. Mr. MT was in the fight for his life with cancer. I could see how, as I heard the news, all the pain starting to unfold. I had not believed he was going to die and when that day came, it was as though nothing else had mattered. I could not control my emotions; they were tearing me apart. As I watched the "movie" in horror, although I knew I had already lived through these times, it was the first time I saw the rollercoaster of emotions, see that I had no control and tears were rolling down my face. It was necessary to complete the study, at times though I wanted to stop, but I knew I must keep watching, so I did. The worst part was not that I lost Mr. MT, it was how, even with my depression at the highest and most harmful, I still could not bring myself to reach out for help. I had let this emotion stay at the highest levels of my current "ruler effect" theory, although I did start, once again, taking antidepressants. I do feel that medications can help, but they are a band aid solution, not the cure or the answer to control depression. Although there is no cure, in my head there had to be a better way to deal with depression, so the next time I could be ready. Unfortunately, I wasn't, depression was once again coming for me, and this time it would almost cost me my family and my life. Soon, the worst time of my life was coming, and I could see that I was in no way ready for it. After three years, I had started to deal with the death of Mr. MT, only because time had passed, but I was not ready to deal with losing anyone else so soon, still having many bad days after the death of Mr. MT. I had never really, dealt with how his death had impacted my life. It was easier to leave it in the back of my mind, like I did with all my feelings for most of my life.

CHAPTER TWENTY

THE CALL CAME AT 5:30 PM. I WAS IN the kitchen with my wife when my phone rang. My father was calling. I answered, thinking it was odd because it was always my mother who called. I asked my dad what was up. He said "Tristan your mom is dead." Thus, began the worst eight months of my life. I could not stop feeling depressed, I was in complete and utter chaos. It almost killed not only me, but everyone in my family. When it was time for my mom's funeral I felt like I wasn't able to show, or deal with, my feelings. Soon after, the wheels came off, feeling nothing but chaos in my mind. I was unable to process my feelings and that's when everything was racing to the highest levels on the scale of what I now call the ruler. I hit that moment of inertia which was the worst free fall of my life, and when the chaos settled eight months later, it had been devastating to my life, my family and my friends. So, when the "movie" turned off, my life went on again. There was no "movie", it's only a metaphor, a very necessary and real rough ride of emotions, but I had to see my life play out and, believe me, in every way, it had been helpful. After I was done writing down all the episodes, I had the insight into every aspect of my depression. I had survived the ride, and although at first I had been afraid to bring up all the emotional times, I could now see where and when the levels where exploding and when they were expelled. It was vital, it was needed and the more I watched the easier it was getting. I only wish I had done it at the beginning, but even at this point, I was still not where I felt that I could rest. I needed more and when I told my wife and talked to MF about what I had done, they were both amazed, however, I explained, I still needed more information. The only way to ascertain this information, was to talk to people like myself and MF. He thought it was great, my wife, not so much as she figured I would fall back into depression. I could see her point, but I had to determine how to find out what made other people's depression work, before I could develop a way to control my own depression. At first I was doing it for myself and my friends, now, at this point, I determined I wanted to write my book. I wasn't sure how to start this process, so after further thought, I realized I would tell people that I was doing research into the world of depression and to my surprise many people offered to give me information. I spent about three months interviewing many depressed individuals, as well as many that felt that they were not experiencing depression. What I learned was astonishing about how many different levels people had and I was seeing the future through all these people. I won't divulge their names of course, because names aren't important, their stories are. When I thought that I had accumulated enough information, I put it all on my desk, uncertain about how to proceed. I went through about two hundred interviews and wasn't sure how I was going to process all their stories, so I came up with a system A B C D E. A: being the people that felt they only had a few bouts of depression; B: still not depressed but more often than the A's; C: more occurrences, but still manageable; D: more days being depressed and tougher to deal with and finally E: what I called living in an ongoing depressed state of life.

I was getting closer to where I wanted to be and when I finally understood the information that I had right in front of me, I was ecstatic. I came to realize that, although we all experience some form of depression, not all of us live continuously depressed. The difference between A and E, was like the distance between the Sun and the Earth. You can feel the Sun, you can see it, but it is so far away you can't touch it and that's what I figured out. Let's say Earth is the beginning and the Sun is the where depression lives. Why would anyone want to live on the Sun, if you would melt and disappear? In my past, I had wished that I could disappear, this is simply what it feels like to be in the mind of the deeply depressed, and that's why I must share my findings and my opinion. Once again, I make no claims to be a doctor or in any way a professional. I wasn't happy just being able to say to myself, well it's okay to stay in the depressed state and accept that I have a chemical imbalance ergo I have irreversible mental illness. Yes, that is the cause, that it would have been okay to just keep living this way, but that wasn't for me.

CHAPTER TWENTY-ONE

MY CONCLUSION WAS THAT THERE are many levels of depression which, like DNA, is different for everyone. It's your mind and no one persons mind works the same. For most, depression can be triggered by deaths, finances, relationships or whatever obstacles come their way, simply because their mind is wired differently. In my life, I had financial success, but that was it. I struggled with all the rest and, as the result of my study, I knew, for myself, first I needed to devise a self-help program.

I felt that although I knew there was no cure for the depressed state, I was not going to be condemned to live any more of my life in the state I found in the "movie" of my life. Again, although it's a metaphor, it was awesome to finally feel like Aladdin and the Magic Carpet Ride. I would spot where I could store all the negative energy and when I realized this, I talked to friends or family, explaining there would be no damage. The times that I would ignore my feelings, the levels of depression would climb to their highest, a point where you could not anticipate when, where and how the release would come. I have started using my theory and it's been two years with my depression, in what I call, a controlled state. I am providing you with the graphs and further explanations in more detail over the next few pages. As the picture became clearer, I shared what I was thinking with MF and my wife, thinking to myself how was I going to explain my findings. I was thinking of all the readings that I researched and thought, first to find peace and happiness, I had to think about where I am the happiest and at peace. It was beside my family, friends and the golf course, where I could see there was utter happiness, where I felt at peace with everything. That's when I found myself putting golf and depression together, with what is called the moment of inertia. In golf, it's simple, it's when the club head meets the ball and jumps off the club. Yes, I know you're thinking how are golf and depression in any way similar. I formulated that in golf as you pull the club back and you change the angle, you begin the downswing toward the point where the club meets ball, that's inertia. The further you can coil, the steeper the angle and the speed of the downswing, the further the ball goes. That's where, in my theory, they are similar, a part of how I taught myself the danger of allowing the ruler to get to the furthest point, then experience the release and the lasting destruction. That's how I came up with all the research and self-healing, to get not only the understanding of depression, but also how to control my mind.

CHAPTER TWENTY-TWO

NOW THAT I HAD FOUND WHAT I needed to start my ever-lasting control over my depression, first I had to face the fact that I was depressed. I'm not living without control and although medications help, they do not totally control depression. I figured that if I reassured myself with happy times, over and over every day, it would work to lower my reactions, and it has. When I think of happy moments, like being at the golf course, and apply those feelings today, I create a calmness in my mind, and that's when I started to come up with various ways to do that. I'm finding that if I can keep my emotional levels at their lowest point of a depressed state, that works. Now I control and vent right away, and if you are ready to give it a go, I'll show you how. That's what will be coming up next, so stop your depression now. It's within your control and to those who believe it doesn't work well, I'm living proof.

CHAPTER TWENTY-THREE

ALTHOUGH I HAVE ONLY MY THEORY, I truly believe it's a way to understand the inner workings of the mind, the various levels of depression, and I believe that is evident in my findings. There is no scientific proof, just my notes and self-evaluation, that at the root of all my emotion, lays depression. In saying that, I believe being in a depressed state is the catalyst for the anger that I felt as the starting point for my actions of violence, fear and self-loathing. I want to better explain the word catalyst, as the leader that would start my emotions in whatever the situation. I will use football because it was the game I played and loved. Consider the quarterback in my theory, as the catalyst, the leader of the team, not that there aren't any defence leaders, but the quarterback, in my opinion, is the guy that sets the mood for his team right from the get go. Let's say his first pass goes for a touchdown, what elation he fires up in the whole team, thus starting everyone off on the right foot. What happens when the mood is good - it's contagious - the team is fired up and the defence responds in a positive way, maybe gets the ball back after a fumble and emotions run high. Things are so easy to deal with when the brain is letting out joy, all because the quarterback is not playing the game on his own. He may have started the movement of all his teammates towards a positive state of mind and as the catalyst, the leader, emotions were positive. The domino effect right from the beginning of the game, is positive. Now let's look again at the catalyst, the quarterback. On the first play he looks back, sees the open man downfield and throws the pass, except this time the free safety intercepts the football and runs it all the way back for a touchdown. Now the mood has changed, just like the many levels of depression. This result is also contagious, except the catalyst started the game in a negative way, so the defence isn't fired up. They allow more touchdowns, become angry with each other, resulting in the game being a blow-out. It was only one play that changed the emotional outcome of the game into a loss. Strong leaders rally their team to come from behind, and can put the one bad opening play behind them. So, there are, in my mind, keys to understanding how the two parties react in different ways, the way I believe that depression levels get their trigger points. When you start the game or the day, with either positive feelings or negative feelings from the moment you wake up, you need to find a way to remind yourself that everything starts with your mood. Your depression wants to flare up right away, so you must stop it in its tracks. I felt that if I could teach myself positivity, right from the start of every day, then I could control my levels of emotion and that would be the key to finding what I had wanted my entire life. I may have been born with depression, but only I could lead my "team" to success, so now I needed to find the formula to start each day in a positive state. How I was going to do that was the million-dollar question, so I started thinking that if I could write it down, maybe then I could follow it as part of my daily regimen. Like the quarterback, I needed to have a game plan. If I threw a touchdown I would kick start the right emotions in a positive game, the game of keeping my level of depression at its lowest point. In doing so, my defence would, in theory, be stronger. If the offence was winning the game, controlled the ball, then the defence would not always be engaged and when it was in the game, the lead would be so big, the defence would have so much energy, that it could keep the depression team at bay.

CHAPTER TWENTY-FOUR

AS I SAT AT MY DESK FOR A WHILE, I knew that in order, to start every day positively, I needed to think about how being on the golf course was where I was in my most tranquil state. I needed to develop a way to recreate that feeling all the time, so the quarterback that is the start of all my emotion, could always throw the ball to the open receiver. I wrote down 6 steps and started to put my theories to work, sharing them with MF and within a few days I felt like I could take on the world of depression. MF and I used these 6 steps every day. It's not like I'm under the impression that I have cured my depression or MF's, but I can deal with my emotions. Controlling them is now so much easier, at their various stages. Over the last two years, it has been put to the test. I can now stop my levels of depression from escalating right at the point I feel the anger or sadness coming. I simply go right to the beginning of my 6 steps and instantly start to gain control, knowing that, if I remember to keep this as a part of the way I live, I feel that depression, at the lowest levels, is like not having it at all. I know I can't change the inner working of my mind but I can control it. Just two years ago I couldn't even say the word depression, let alone think that I would be able to write about it, tell anyone that wants to talk about it. I am a depressed man, but I feel the more I say it, the more I talk about it, it no longer has control of my life. I am now in control, armed with the knowledge of how to use that control. Depression tried to ruin every day of my life, but now I feel empowered. I stood up and took control of my mind and my body and I know that you and anyone else can take control of their life too. You can't take depression out of your mind, no it's there, but you can respect depression and tell it that it also needs to respect you. I'm not saying I'm the master of depression, I'm just telling you what has led me to a life worth living and that I believe those same 6 steps can help you. I'm not selling any programs or asking people to sign up to any website. I only have one reason for reaching out with my book and that is, I have lived in a depressed state of mind for most of my life, and if my book can help even one person to find the light that leads to internal peace, then there's my payoff.

These are my six steps for dealing with everyday depression. It is what I do every morning and when I need it:

1 Recognize

2 Realize

3 Release

4 Reward

5 Rejoice

6 Repeat

Stages and percentage
levels of depression

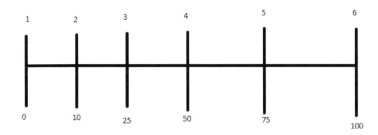

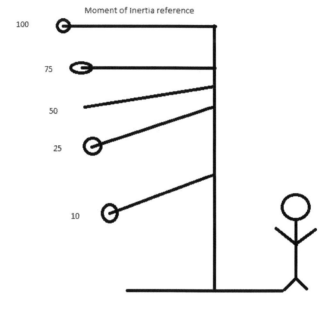

Moment of inertia reference

CHAPTER TWENTY-FIVE

THE FIRST STEP IS TO RECOGNIZE THAT
you are living in a depressed state and accept the
fact that depression is what is making you tired,
achy and only seeing the darkness, not the light.
Tell yourself every day, that you will be okay and
not to be ashamed, that it is not your fault, and you
need to speak and seek help to release the pain that
has crippled you. That will not only start you on
the road to feeling better, but will empower you to
do whatever it takes, to understand that depression

affects everything, and that emotions rock your life. Recognize that depression affects everything you say and, at its worst, blocks any sources of positive feelings in any shape or form, of happiness. Recognize that you need to look in the mirror and identify that you are tired in every possible way, that you are making the choice to stop the path of depression and that you don't want this life any more. Recognize that you are not simply ignoring the depression in your mind and body that you felt you had no control over, because you know that is not the way it has to be. Recognize that there is a way to stop depression at the beginning signs and you are not going to let it just stay at the back of your mind.

I am proud of you and now you're ready to start the next step.

Step 2 is the hardest and the toughest hurdle you will face. It is realization. You need to realize the fear you have, opening up to yourself and others by telling them that you are depressed, that you have concealed your depression from everyone, that you have been dealing with depression alone for so long in fear and it was hell. You must realize you were dealing with depression alone, feeling that you were the only one that was living this way. Recognize that you have been so afraid to share your living hell with anyone, because you thought they would simply not care. You must realize that you need to talk and share your feelings, because it is no longer okay to keep depression to yourself and realize that you need to get over this fear, a huge and scary thing to do, but it's time. Step 2 is vital to finding your own salvation. It is reaffirming to the success of your control of depression, that you are ready to take this next step. Sharing is realizing that you are ready to move forward and are starting to deal with what most people are afraid of, letting friends and family know that you have been living in pain and it has been affecting your quality of life. Realization is the hardest step to deal with and if you feel that it was what was holding you back, well if you are reading step 2, feel that you have realized and that the next steps are easier and rewarding.

Step 3, release, is my favorite. This is where you seek the help of professional guidance, a best friend or clergyman. This step is where you start to feel stronger and don't feel afraid to share your feelings because, I'm telling you, release is the best and most freeing thing you can do to let depression leave your mind and soul. If you feel that someone might be negative, say who the fuck cares what others think. Release comes when you can say to yourself or anyone in ear shot, I'm depressed and I'm beating it to the back of my mind. It's so amazing because you are finally taking control of your mind and body and nothing feels better. The more you let it out, the simpler it is to do what you thought was so hard.

Not only are you telling everyone that you chose your destiny, you're telling yourself that you aren't going to let depression run whenever it feels like ruining your day. Release feels so good, like the first sunlight of spring, suddenly it's wonderful to see colours so bright, and everything in your mind is clear. You want to live every day this way and I know that it may sound corny, but I'm telling you, it's how I see it and I how live every day now. It's up to you to see it for yourself. I hope that you do and when you do, you are ready for the next and even easier step.

Step 4 is reward. I love this step because it means that you are almost home to finding lasting happiness. I don't mean that reward is to go out and buy a new set of golf clubs, a new car or go on a major shopping spree. Reward in this context, is the action of going out and doing things that you can now do with your new outlook on life. With the new found control of my depressed state of mind it was, for me, like being a kid in a candy store. I remember how I used to buy things which, at first made me feel great, but it was just masking the depression in my mind. Material things don't make you happy in the long run because you are still depressed. Buying things will not help you deal with your state of mind, so sooner or later, you slip back to the depressed state. When you are living in a good space in your mind, material things are not so important in your life. I can remember the rewarding feeling of just going to the park and playing with my children, looking at the garden and even finding golf more enjoyable. My outlook was filled with promise and joy and when my wife and family could see my outlook had changed, the reward was a better more fulfilling life.

Step 5 is, rejoice. Well, congratulations, you got to the easiest step. By this point I found life so much easier to accept, I am content and finding my life filled with understanding that the life I had struggled with, is now firmly in the back ground, I could rejoice. I knew depression would always be in my mind, but the controls I had taught myself using the 6 steps was the necessary tool to keep it where it needed to be, in the furthest part of my mind. I also knew, that whenever I needed to talk about my struggles of living with depression, I wasn't in any way afraid to do it. Rejoice is knowing that I could do it and, to be honest, I can now say the word depression the same way I say golf. I have total control of the way I deal with my feelings and when I feel that something is going in the wrong direction, I take the necessary steps to recognize, realize, release and re-find my comfort zone. I'm not any smarter or braver than you, just simply aware of not allowing depression to control me

Step 6 is repeat and in many ways, the most important. Using step 6 when you wake up in the morning is like brushing your teeth or washing your hair. Recite in your head or out loud, repeating the six steps. You think it might be unnecessary, but it's vital. It reaffirms the steps to yourself, so that in your day, if you feel that depression is just around the corner, you're ready and believe me depression is always lurking in the background, ready to wreak havoc. That's what depression is. It sits and waits for you to allow it to cause you to suffer you, so be ready to use the 6 steps to success.

For myself, these steps have been vital because, in my case, I have to stay on guard so I don't allow myself the luxury to be caught off guard. I like being happy and in control of my mind and yes, it can be tough at times, but feeling depressed is a much tougher emotion to deal with. I know some of you might think that this seems crazy, but I'm just letting you understand that this is the way I stay in line, and what I will need to do for the rest of my life. It works and whether you try it or not is your choice, but I'm telling you, it has changed the way I live my life and I know my family and friends are living proof that it's the reason I have found peace.

CHAPTER TWENTY-SIX

INERTIA

I NEEDED TO SHOW MY WIFE AND MF

the formula and the way I use it to explain the effect

of the moment of inertia, the way I believe it led to

so many manic and destructive paths in my life. It

was so much easier to draw the movement then to

just talk about it, that after doing so, I could get

their opinion and be there to watch their reaction.

Using the dictionary, I found the definition of

inertia: the moment of inertia is Kg plus m2 s. To simplify it, mass times velocity and speed at a steeper angle curbs more speed and even more force. That's how I came up with using this word to explain the dangers of allowing depression to rise to the highest levels where it starts the downward escalation, and that's why you must stay away from this feeling of depression.

The only time I heard this action of MOI, the Moment Of Inertia, is when golf club manufacturers talk about their club's MOI. The greater MOI leads to getting your ball to travel longer, and I put that same theory to better use to show the dangers of the effect of depression. These are my theories and not that of a lab study, using my own life experiences and that of watching life through my eyes. One day, I hope that I can make my studies known and put to the test throughout the world, not for anything more than helping others like myself. The formula is simple and I have used MOI to further understand how I had no control over my depression. Bottling up my depressions was like boiling water but, unlike water that dissipates the longer it boils, I was not allowing depression to leave my mind so, at the point of boiling, I was losing all control of the state of my mind. That's why I left it, continuing and continuing, until I couldn't stop the MOI in my mind and sooner or later the top would come off. That's when my favorite quote was actually the same way I was living my life over and over again. The quote says the definition of insanity is doing the same thing over and over and expecting a different result. Hopefully you can understand what I am trying to get at. In theory, you have a ruler and the digits range from 0 to 100, so let's take the first increment of numbers, where I feel that most people have dealt with mild depression. For example, when something goes wrong at work or other simple things, they are usually dealt with causing little or no long term emotional repercussions and would fall in the range of 0 to 10. I believe the individuals that don't have ongoing depression when life gives them an upsetting event, accept these events as a part of everyday life. Let me give you an example. If you took an object such as 2 cups of coffee and moved them gently together from 0cm to 10cm, there would be very minimal movement, not enough to cause any damage to the cups. Why? There was so little travel and speed from the start of the movement to the short trip back from 10cm to 0cm, that the impact of the action was almost nothing to minimal. In my study, this is a safe amount of depression, where the anger or emotional state is controlled and at very manageable levels. It's where I live right now.

Level 2 involves people who have a couple of episodes a month, more easily depressed than those in Stage 1, and fall on the ruler in the range of 0 cm to 25 cm. At this level the fallout is minimal. Again, using the coffee cup theory, although it would have a little more effect, these people continue to control their emotions, still in the good zone.

Level 3 occurs when you move any further than 25 cm. I believe that is when the depression is present more, as a sufferer of a full time depressed state, and the further you move down the ruler the harder it is to realize your state of mind. The longer you let depression simmer, the more agitated you become. Keep in mind, the more you stay depressed, and the more things that go wrong in your life and mind, the more you are moving closer to the danger levels, where control is hard. You become so sad that common sense is hard to achieve, and the angle of your travel starts to change, increasing the speed flows with a much greater force than you realized. Once your mind can no longer handle the resulting anger and fear, every emotion leading to major depression is at its most dangerous level for you, or anyone in your path then the moment of inertia is triggered. I have seen the events that result when depression falls and you can't stop the momentum. Hopefully you have not done too much destruction to yourself, or anyone that you unleashed on, because depression does not, in any way, give you the right to cause harm to anyone. During the highest level of depression, you are always living in a depressed state of mind and I know that's where I had lived most of my life, hard just to wake up and get through each day. I feel that I stole so much, from so many people that tried to love me, always pushing them away, simply because that was easier to do. I could never talk about myself and hid behind the Bammer, who didn't accept depression, didn't give a shit about his feelings or, most of the time, anyone else's feelings. That would work for a while, but eventually it would come crashing down harder than I could never imagine, almost costing me my life on more than one occasion. You need to love yourself before anyone else can love you. Mental health is so difficult to admit to, it's hard to deal with depression on your own. Doing it alone is an arduous battle, you need some help and you need to find it now. If you have someone that can walk down the road with you, it will keep you standing up, be your leaning post or rock. I had my wife, MF, and all my family, making it easier for me. I was determined not to let depression lead my life any longer and although it started with that decision, it was nice to have someone there for support throughout my journey. Today I feel at peace and I'm not afraid to deal with my mental state. I had been depressed for so long, but I guess I needed to go through it in order to help anyone that asks for my help. You need to recognize that you need and want help, but I believe that anyone can do it. They say that depression can't be stopped, it's hereditary, but you have the choice of whether to let it hold you hostage, or to control it. I lived with depression almost my whole life until I hit rock bottom, but I have controlled it for two years with almost no hiccups. Don't let yourself or anyone else tell you otherwise, because I'm telling you, that is utter bullshit. I have made it my life's mission, to reach out, write this book and help anyone who seeks my help. People say you're not a doctor or have any kind of licence, and I simply reply, you're right. I'm not asking for money or gifts of any kind. I'm a recovering sufferer of depression and I have walked in those shoes, so I'm not asking for advice. I think I can recount my story, tell them that they aren't alone, and I would love to see them happy. Whether doctors might think it's bullshit, they can't tell me whether I'm for real or not, because I'm not here for doubters, only believers that want to find what I have found. Depression doesn't own me, I own it, and I can tell you that it feels amazing. I can only hope that everyone in the world experiencing depression will someday find their peace, because they deserve that. When I was doing my studies, I found out that my family, on my mother's side, had a long history of mental illness, with many members of my family on antidepressants, and here I thought I was special. It then became even more imperative that I find success, in case one of my children would struggle with that same pattern of life. That's when I felt that I needed to find a way to explain to them how it worked, and how they could deal with it. My youngest child wasn't even ten, so knowing how young I was when I started to feel depression, I came up with the ruler, the chain, the ball, and the MOI graph that are now going to be explained. Look them over and then I will share the findings and graphs.

I believe that the list is so long of how many countless atrocities have been caused because of the core state of depression at the MOI, so that is why I designed a model of the MOI that I could show my children. I had to show them what their father had had for most of his life and that after talking about depression, I could show them the model of the MOI, how it would feel to not have control and the dangers at the various levels. I believe that is how all depression levels can be explained, and to be honest, when I used a ball and watched at various levels, it was so educational to see the effects to the ball and thinking wow, I wish I would have come up with this a long time ago. Imagine you have a 100-foot-long chain, and you attach it to a pole 95 feet in the air. At one end, you put a 10-lb steel ball to test the theory, the ball representing your brain, and using the numbers I gave you on the ruler, move the ball in the increments that I talked about, so 0 to 10, 10 to

25 and 25 to 50. By the time you get to 50, both the angle and the arc change and when the ball is at the top level of the pole, it's what I called the depressed state, and when released from there, it's the most dangerous and the most destructive. Imagine what damage, with that mass and the speed, using only 10 lbs of weight, it would cause to a wood door. It would be smashed to pieces! That's what my brain felt like, every time I allowed it to stay in a depressed state for so long without dealing with it. I watched the model at all the levels they had on there and the effect of the MOI when it was at what I considered 100 percent of the depressed state, the most dangerous level, not just for you, but for anyone who is unlucky enough to be in your path. That's why I built the model in my backyard and that's why I want you to see that by not finding help, this could be you. Trust me, it's not great and it's tough to always need to pick up all the pieces after all the destruction you cause, in some

cases people commit suicide, or hurt people around them that have no reason to feel the wrath that you feel, thinking in some way it was going to make your hurt go away. You couldn't be more wrong! I hope that, in some way, these findings will help you to see where your levels are, and if you're anywhere near 50, GET HELP NOW. You will find that life can get better, even if, right now, you feel alone, helpless, confused, or that no-one cares. I've been there and know all too well what that feels like. There were times when I felt like death was my only option and I am so happy to have been a coward and not gone through with it. I admitted that I needed help and then, I decided I was ready to find a way to control the depression that had made my life a living hell.

CHAPTER TWENTY-SEVEN

IN MY EYES, AT THE CORE OF IT ALL, I believe depression has always been the catalyst of all my emotions. Most of the world has control over their emotions, but from what I had read, there are around 300 million people experiencing depression. I'm not sure, personally I feel that number could be understated. I would estimate double that number, but unless we contact every human in the world, I'll have to agree the original number is good enough. Imagine if all those sufferers could reach the number

0 on the ruler. I know I'm a big dreamer, but I'll keep dreaming. Through all my life, dealing with the feelings of depression, there were so many heartbreaks and feelings I was hiding, and using a dual personality under the nickname the Bammer, was so unhealthy. If this is how you are living, I know it feels safe, but it's not good for you in any way. I understand because I lived that way, so you should not follow that example, it's just masking your problems. If I could turn back the clock of my life, to the first time I experienced depressive feelings at the age of 5, knowing what I know now, maybe I could have changed so many hardships. I know that is impossible so I must look back at it to understand how precious life is, but having mental health issues at such a young age, how would I have known that I was depressed. I never really, heard about depression until I was about 20, and it was tough growing up through those early years. I had

always felt the emotions but would never admit that I was continually unhappy. I was considered tough, so how could I tell anyone what I felt like. I had to keep all those feelings locked up, for no-one else to see. I couldn't be seen as weak and so, by the time I was 30, I was the Bammer and how could that cool cat feel anything like depression. That's when my levels would climb and not subside, because I had no control of the situation. I couldn't stop it because, like the 10-lb ball at the top of its height and at the speed it travels at, depression only comes to a stop when it slows, having already destroyed everything in its path. For some suffers it just can't be fixed, because in some rages they cause destruction to the human race, by killing others. It's bad enough to hurt you and that's why you can't hide from yourself and you can't feel suicide is the only answer. That's only depression at its worst and it's time to take care of yourself. I know I repeat those 6 words to control my depression, help my levels, as well as a few more key words and why I have shared this with the readers of my book. Hopefully lol. The more you say the words, the more comfortable it is to say them, and the more you can deal with the emotions that the words bring you. I had a hard time with the word depression in any forum at all, but I feel that understanding the words helps you to believe you can find the way to mental peace.

I hope that what I have shared with you not only helps, but convinces you that you too can find the courage to make change. When you deal with how you feel, it will make other things better, because a healthy mind is so creative. This is all I want. If one person lets me know that all my stories, findings or diagrams have helped them, that all I lived and suffered through helped you, then I can feel that this book was a success. I hope all sufferers, at whatever level, one day find the road to controlling their depression. If I had one wish, it would be that depression would not exist, but until then, I'll fight and if anyone needs to talk to me I'll never say no.

FINAL CHAPTER

MY JOURNEY HAS BEEN LONG, AT TIMES
it felt impossible to go on for more days and nights
then I care to remember. Through many roads filled
with darkness when I felt that I would never again
see the light, to the worst days when my future was
in the grasp of the grim-reaper, caused by an illness
that almost took my life, to that point when I found
that I could stand up and fight. I was blessed to have
such a wonderful wife, family and best friend in MF,
that a man could have. I started first by healing my

body and then my mind, although I had spent almost eight months trying to end my life. Thank God I found the will. I'm aware that DEPRESSION IS ALWAYS WAITING TO RELEASE ITS ANGER AND HATRED and that's all good. I'M ALWAYS READY TO FIGHT BACK, by having control of my own mind. Depression is not welcome and that puts a smile on my face. Awareness is now at the highest levels. They are finally taking depression seriously, that it leads to many facets of crime and I'm glad that it's not being shoved under the carpet any more, that when it's at its highest point it's as dangerous as a gun in the hands of a madman.

I hope that life finds everyone well and that, in some way, I've made your life a little bit easier. I have been writing this book for the few or many that want to know what I say, and it's been tough and the road bumpy. I know some people may think, who is this man to tell us how and why it is vital to control all emotions. Well see, that's the point. When you control your mind, what people say to hurt or discredit you, really doesn't matter, because you know why. I wrote this for you!

I was lost and now I am found

I have lived but I have not lived

I have loved but I have not loved

But because of you I am alive

With you I know I will soar

These are the words I had tattooed on me. So, go live, love and soar like never before.

Printed in the United States
By Bookmasters